# How We Use

# Coal

Chris Oxlade

## www.raintreepublishers.co.uk
Visit our website to find out more information about **Raintree** books.

To order:
☎ Phone 44 (0) 1865 888112
▤ Send a fax to 44 (0) 1865 314091
▭ Visit the Raintree bookshop at **www.raintreepublishers.co.uk** to browse our catalogue and order online.

First published in Great Britain by Raintree,
Halley Court, Jordan Hill, Oxford OX2 8EJ,
part of Harcourt Education.
Raintree is a registered trademark of
Harcourt Education Ltd.

© Harcourt Education Ltd 2004
First published in paperback in 2005
The moral right of the proprietor has been asserted.

Editorial: Nick Hunter
Design: Kim Saar
Picture Research: Heather Sabel and Amor
   Montes de Oca
Production: Alex Lazarus

Originated by Ambassador Litho Ltd.
Printed and bound in China by South China
Printing Company

ISBN 1 844 43260 2 (hardback)
08 07 06 05 04
10 9 8 7 6 5 4 3 2 1

ISBN 1 844 43270 X (paperback)
09 08 07 06 05
10 9 8 7 6 5 4 3 2 1

**British Library Cataloguing in Publication Data**
Oxlade, Chris
How We Use Coal. - (Using Materials)
553.2'4
A full catalogue record for this book is available from the British Library.

**Acknowledgements**
The publishers would like to thank the following for permission to reproduce photographs:
Ace Library pp. **8**(Gayle Mault), **24**; Brand X Pictures (David Wasserman) p. **16**; Corbis pp. **4** (Larry Lee Photography), **7** (Hulton-Deutsch Collection), **9** (H.David Seawell), **12** (Andy Butler/Eye Ubiquitous), **18** (George H. Huey), **19** (James A. Sugar), **20** (AFP), **26** (Michael St. Maur Sheil), **28** (Lester Lefkowitz), **29** (Will and Deni McIntyre); Foodpix (Dennis Gottlieb) p. **21**; Image Works (Lee Snider) p. **27**; John T. Fowler p. **13**; Meonshore Studios Limited (Mike French) p. **22**; Peter and Georgina Bowater p. **23**; Photo Researchers Inc. (Hiene Scheebeli) p. **5**; Science Photo Library (Cordelia Molloy) p. **17**; Visuals Unlimited pp. **6** (Steve McCutcheon), **10** (Steve McCutcheon), **11** (Science VU), **14** (Inga Spence), **15** (John D. Cunningham), **25** (Science VU).

Cover photographs reproduced with permission of Corbis (top) and Photo Researchers Inc. (C. Molloy) (bottom).

# Contents

Any words appearing in bold, **like this**, are explained in the Glossary.

# Coal and its properties

All the objects we use are made from materials. Coal is a material. Most coal is used as **fuel** because it burns well. **Coal tar** is one of the materials we get from coal. We use coal tar in some soap because it can be good for skin. It is also used for making roofs because it is **waterproof**.

Coal is a type of rock. We get it from the ground.

We burn more coal for heating and making **electricity** than any other fuel.

**Properties** tell us what a material is like. Coal is a **solid**. It is black or dark brown. Coal is brittle. This means it breaks apart easily and crumbles into coal dust. We get other materials by splitting up coal into different parts.

## Don't use it!

*The different properties of materials make them useful for different jobs. For example, we would not use coal to make containers. They would break easily and make the things inside dirty.*

# Where does coal come from?

Coal is a **natural** material. The coal we use today was made millions of years ago. When bushes, tropical trees, and other plants died they fell into **swamps**. They were gradually buried by new rocks. Over millions of years the dead plants were turned into coal. Some coal is made from plants that lived before the dinosaurs! We call coal a **fossil fuel**.

This seam of black coal in Arkansas, USA, is trapped by layers of other rocks.

A hundred years ago steam ships ran on coal. Stokers shovelled coal into fires to keep the engines running.

## Coal in history

*Coal was burned as a **fuel** in China more than 3000 years ago. It became a much more important material about 250 years ago. Then coal started to be used as a fuel in steam engines, and for making large quantities of iron.*

We find coal in layers called **seams**. There are other layers of rocks above and below the coal. Scientists called geologists try to work out where there might be coal seams hidden underground. They drill holes into the ground to see if they are right.

# Mining coal

Getting coal from the ground is called coal **mining**. Sometimes we find coal **seams** on the surface or only a little way underground. We get this coal by surface mining. Miners break up the coal with drills and explosives and scoop up the lumps of coal with diggers. When a coal seam is deep underground miners have to dig a hole called a shaft. They use drills and huge buckets to lift the coal to the surface.

This machine digs deep underground. It breaks coal from a coal seam.

Coal is broken into small lumps and washed after it is mined.

We find coal in the ground all over the world, but we cannot use all of it. Sometimes coal seams are not big enough to be worth digging up. Sometimes they are too far down to reach.

## Danger in the mines

*Going deep underground to dig out coal can be dangerous. There are often* **gases** *in mines that can explode. Rock can fall on top of miners, and water can flood into mines.*

# Types of coal

There are three types of coal. The **properties** of each type are slightly different. Each one also contains a different amount of a substance called **carbon**. Carbon is the part of coal that burns.

**Anthracite** is a type of coal that is nearly all carbon. Anthracite is hard, black and shiny. It is difficult to light, but it burns very well. It makes lots of heat and hardly any smoke or smell.

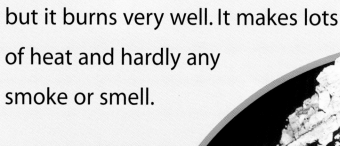

Anthracite is black and shiny.

There is lots of bituminous coal for us to dig up.

About nine-tenths of all the coal we use is called **bituminous** coal. It contains slightly less carbon than anthracite but burns well and makes a little smoke.

The third type of coal is called **lignite**. Only about half of lignite is carbon. Lignite is brown and crumbly. It makes much less heat than anthracite or bituminous coal, and is very smoky. Lignite is burned in homes and power stations.

# Coal for heat

The most important **property** of coal is that it burns well. When it burns it gives off lots of heat. This is why we use coal as a **fuel**. About three-quarters of all the coal that is **mined** from the ground is burned as fuel. Most of this coal is burned in power stations to make **electricity**. Lumps of coal burn slowly so they keep giving off heat for a long time.

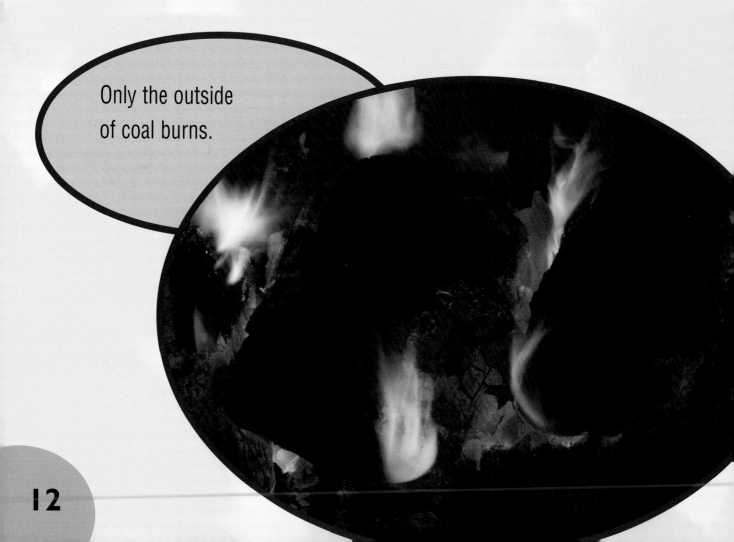

Only the outside of coal burns.

After coal has burned grey dust called ash is left over. We have to get rid of the ash before we burn more coal.

In some countries coal is also a fuel for cooking and heating in homes, offices and factories. The best type of coal for heating and cooking is **anthracite**. It can be used on open fires, in stoves or in central-heating boilers.

## Don't use it!

*In some places coal is not used for heating homes as much as it was many years ago. It has been replaced with cleaner fuels such as **natural gas**.*

# Coal for power

About three-quarters of all coal is burned in power stations to make **electricity** for homes, schools, offices, factories, street lighting and trains. Most power stations burn **bituminous** coal because there is plenty of it. It also burns faster than **anthracite** and gives out lots of heat. **Lignite** gives out much less heat than bituminous coal. It is only used in power stations that are very close to lignite mines.

A power station burns hundreds of tonnes of coal every day. The coal is brought by train.

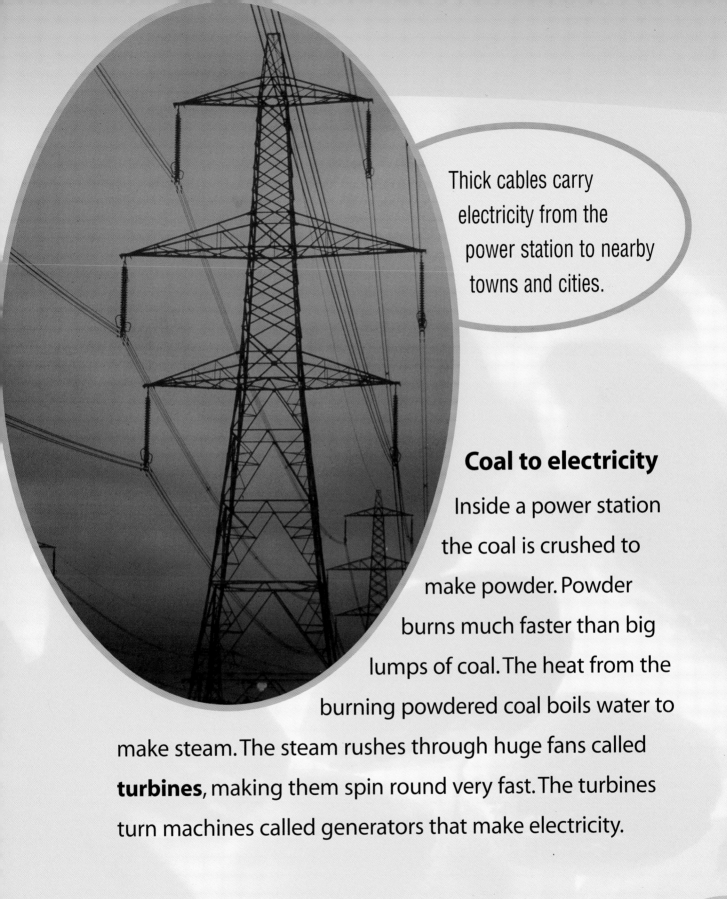

Thick cables carry electricity from the power station to nearby towns and cities.

## Coal to electricity

Inside a power station the coal is crushed to make powder. Powder burns much faster than big lumps of coal. The heat from the burning powdered coal boils water to make steam. The steam rushes through huge fans called **turbines**, making them spin round very fast. The turbines turn machines called generators that make electricity.

# Smokeless coal

When coal burns it makes smoke that rises into the air. The smoke looks grey because it contains tiny bits of **carbon** that did not burn properly. If there are a lot of coal fires close together the smoke can cause thick fog called **smog**. Smog is dangerous for people who have asthma and other breathing problems.

Bits of unburnt coal and ash are carried upwards by the hot rising **gases** from the fire.

Coal that burns with very little smoke is better for the environment.

To stop smog happening many towns and cities around the world have banned people from burning coal that makes smoke. Instead, people must burn smokeless coal. **Bituminous** coal is made smokeless by heating it up but not letting it burn. This gets rid of the substances in the coal that cause smoke. **Anthracite** naturally produces only a little smoke.

# Coal for moving

A hundred years ago nearly all trains and ships had steam engines. The steam engines worked using heat from coal. Coal was burned on a fire underneath a tank of water called a boiler. The heat from the coal boiled the water to make steam and the steam pushed and pulled on **pistons**. In a steam train the pistons turned the wheels. In a ship the pistons turned the propeller.

These are steam trains. Steam from the boilers pushes and pulls the pistons to make the wheels turn.

These men are shovelling coal into the firebox of a steam train.

There are still some steam trains around the world. Modern trains run on diesel engines or **electricity**. The power for electric trains can still come from burning coal, but in a power station many kilometres away. Most modern ships have diesel engines or use oil instead of coal to heat their boilers.

## Don't use it!

*Coal burns well, but slowly. So we cannot use coal for some jobs. For example, we could not use coal instead of petrol in a car engine. It would burn too slowly and clog up the engine.*

# Coal and coke

We do not burn all the coal that is **mined**. Coal is made up of many useful substances. These substances are lost when coal is burned. We get the substances from the coal by heating it in a very hot oven where there is no air. Because there is no air the coal doesn't burn. Lots of hot **gases** come out of the coal instead.

This molten iron was made using coke.

Barbecue fuel is also made from coke.

A dark grey **solid** material is left behind in the oven. It is called coke. Coke is lighter than coal and has small holes in it. Nine-tenths of all the coke made is used as a **raw material** for making iron and steel. The coke is burned in a furnace with iron **ore**. The **carbon** in the coke helps to take out the iron from the ore.

# Coal tar

The **gases** from a coke-making oven do not go to waste. When they cool down they turn into useful materials. **Coal tar** is a black, oily **liquid** made when **bituminous** coal is turned into coke. Coal-tar soap and ointments for itchy skin contain substances from coal tar. Some **fertilizers** that help plants to grow also contain coal tar.

Coal-tar soap can be good for the skin.

This black liquid is called creosote. It comes from coal tar. It helps to stop wood **rotting**.

## Pitch

Pitch is a black **solid** that comes from coal tar. It is sticky and **waterproof**. Builders put pitch on roofs to stop water leaking through. Pitch is also used to make road surfaces. It sticks together the small bits of rock in the road surface and stops water getting into the road.

## Don't use it!

*Coal tar helps to soothe skin problems such as eczema. Many skin ointments contain a little coal tar. We cannot use coal tar straight on to our skin though, because it makes us itch.*

# More fuels from coal

Another **gas** that comes from a coke-making oven is called coal gas. Coal gas burns very well. It is used as a **fuel** to heat the coke-making ovens. Fifty years ago coal gas was supplied to people's houses. It burned in gas stoves for cooking and in gas lamps that lit homes.

These tanks contain coal gas.

This is natural gas burning on a stove. Natural gas replaced coal gas about 50 years ago.

## Changing coal

We can change **solid** coal into gases or **liquids** to burn as fuels. Turning coal into gas is called gasification. Turning coal into liquid is called liquefaction. It makes coal into petrol for engines and fuel oil for heating. At the moment we do not use these processes because we get fuels from crude oil and **natural** gas. We may have to use them eventually, however, because supplies of crude oil and natural gas will run out.

### Don't use it!
*Coal gas burns well but it makes black dust called soot. We now use natural gas instead of coal gas for cooking because natural gas does not make soot.*

# Peat

When plants that live in bogs or **swamps** die their remains fall into the water. They do not completely **rot** away in the water. They are gradually buried under more remains. Over hundreds of years a layer of spongy material builds up. This material is called peat. If peat gets buried under layers of rock it slowly turns to coal.

These workers are digging peat from a peat bog.

Some peat is squashed into handy blocks called peat briquettes.

When peat is dried it burns very well. It is an important **fuel** in a few parts of the world such as Ireland. The peat is dug from a peat bog. It is very wet so it must be dried before it can be burned. Peat is also used as a **fertilizer** because it contains lots of goodness for the soil.

## Don't use it!
*Peat comes from places called peat bogs. They are important* **habitats** *for many plants and animals. Some people think that we should not dig up peat for garden fertilizer. They say we are destroying habitats just to make our plants grow better.*

# Coal and the environment

When coal burns it gives off smoke. Smoke contains tiny bits of unburnt coal that causes **smog** and makes people ill. We can reduce smoke by using smokeless **fuels**. In many power stations the particles are trapped before they can get into the air. This helps to keep the air clean.

We still burn smoky coal in many places. The smoke can travel hundreds of kilometres in the air.

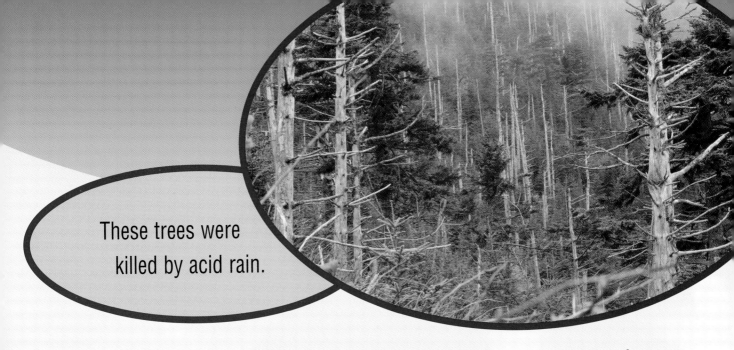

These trees were killed by acid rain.

Burning coal also gives off **gases** that are changing the Earth's atmosphere. One of the gases is carbon dioxide. This is one of the gases causing global warming, which is making our weather change. Coal also contains a lot of a substance called sulphur. When the sulphur gets into the air it turns rain into an **acid**. Acid rain harms trees and wildlife. Modern power stations remove sulphur before it gets into the air.

## Mining

Getting coal from the ground also spoils the environment. **Mines** make the countryside look ugly. Harmful substances are made when coal is cleaned before it is burned. These can get into rivers and poison the wildlife that lives there.

# Find out for yourself

The best way to find out more about coal is to investigate for yourself. If you use coal at home look at the lumps of coal. One of your relatives might use coal in their home, too. Look out for smoke coming from chimneys during the day, for coal bunkers in gardens, coal wagons and coal depots. How do you think the coal is used? You will find the answers to many of your questions in this book. You can also look in other books and on the Internet.

## Books to read

*Science Answers: Grouping Materials*, Carol Ballard (Heinemann Library, 2003)

*Discovering Science: Matter*, Rebecca Hunter (Raintree, 2003)

*Science Files: Rocks and Minerals*, Steve Parker (Heinemann Library, 2002)

## Using the Internet

Try searching the Internet to find out about things to do with coal. Websites can change, so if the link below no longer works, don't worry. Use a search engine, such as www.yahooligans.com or www.internet4kids.com. For example, you could try searching using the keywords 'smokeless coal', 'asthma' and '**acid** rain'.

## Websites

A great site, which explains all about different materials:
http://www.bbc.co.uk/schools/revisewise/science/materials/

# Glossary

**acid** liquid that eats away at materials

**anthracite** type of coal that contains lots of carbon

**bituminous** type of coal

**carbon** part of coal that burns

**coal tar** black, oily liquid that comes from coal

**electricity** form of energy that flows along wires. Much of the electricity we use at home is made at power stations using heat from burning coal.

**fertilizer** material that contains goodness that plants need to grow better

**fossil fuel** fuel made from the remains of animals and plants that died millions of years ago. Coal, oil and natural gas are fossil fuels.

**fuel** material that burns well, making plenty of heat

**gas** substance that spreads out to fill the space it is in

**habitat** place where an animal or a plant lives. For example, a wood is a habitat.

**lignite** type of coal

**liquid** substance that takes the shape of whatever container it is put into

**mine** place where coal or another material is dug from the ground

**natural** describes anything that is not made by people

**ore** rock from which certain types of metal can be taken

**piston** part of an engine that is moved by steam or burning gas

**property** quality of a material that tells us what it is like. Hard, soft, bendy and strong are all properties.

**raw material** material that is used to make other materials

**rot** to be broken down

**seam** layer of coal under the ground

**smog** thick fog caused by smoke in the atmosphere

**solid** substance that does not flow

**swamp** ground covered in shallow water

**turbine** machine like a propeller that turns when steam flows through it

**waterproof** describes a material that does not let water flow through it

# Index